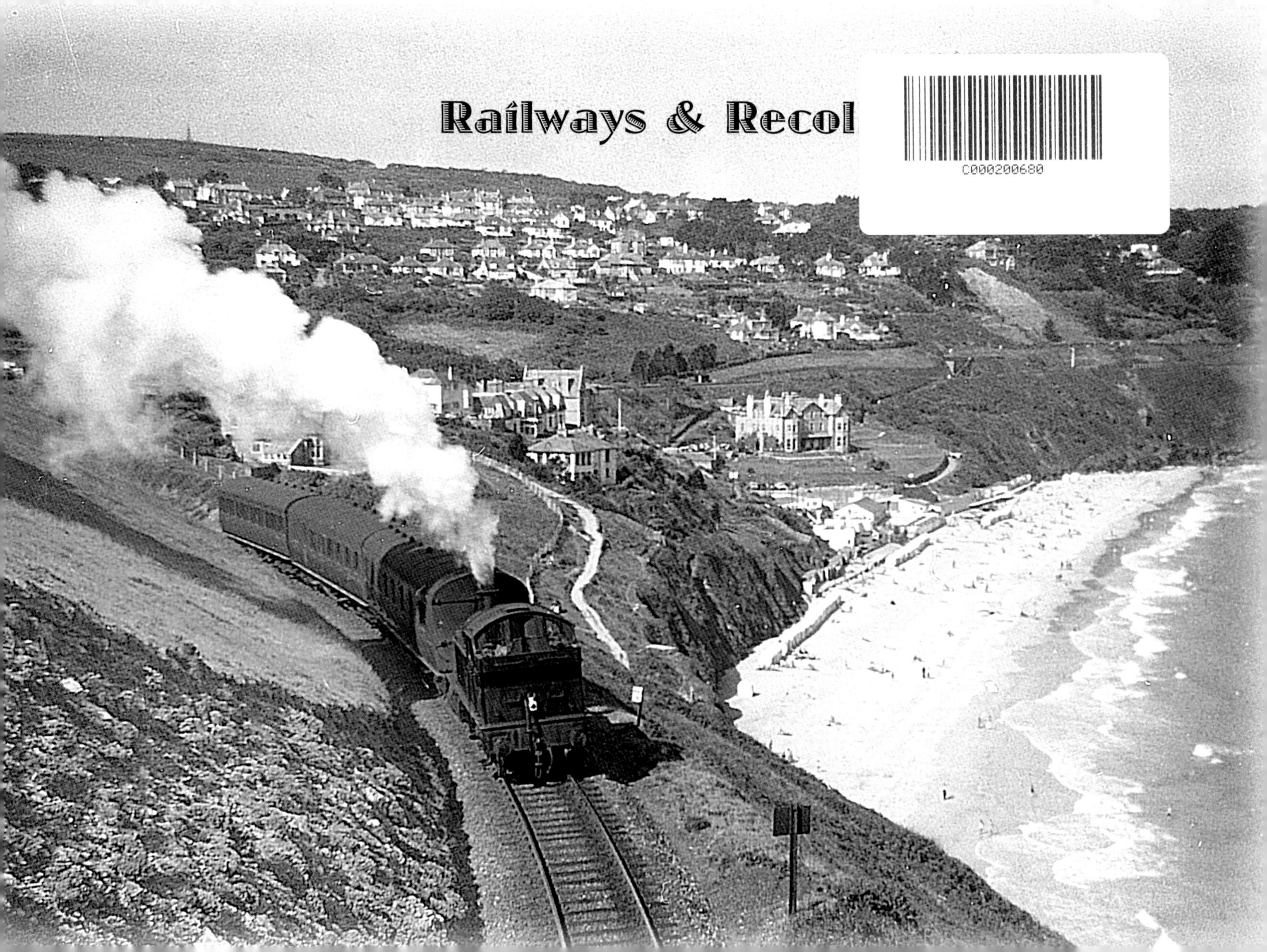
Railways & Recol
C000200680

Contents

Introduction	3
Steam on the Western region	1- 12
Steam in the the Midlands, the North, the South & Scotland	13
The Birmingham area	21
Locomotives on shed	27
Out on the lines	34
Railway Works	38
Wolverton	40
Focus on Whitby	43
Nantybwch	46
Happenings	7, 15, 22, 46
Arrivals & Departures	38
No 1 Records 1957	28

Frontispiece: **CARBIS BAY** For many in the post-War austerity period, summer holidays and trains went hand in hand. Many thousands of holidaymakers travelled to their seaside destinations by rail and this delightful scene from those halcyon days is a typical example of the appeal as well as the practicality of these journeys. On a bight sunny day in September, an unidentified '4500' Class 2-6-2T passes the sands of Carbis Bay, on its way from St Ives to St Erth.

First published in 2008
ISBN 978 1 85794 291 0

Silver Link Publishing Ltd
The Trundle
Ringstead Road
Great Addington
Kettering
Northants NN14 4BW

Tel/Fax: 01536 330588
email: sales@nostalgiacollection.com
Website: www.nostalgiacollection.com
British Library Cataloguing in Publication Data
A catalogue record for this book is available from the British Library.
Printed and bound in Great Britain

Acknowledgements

First and foremost we would like to record our gratitude to the late Ray Ruffell without whom this book would not have been possible. Ray was a railwayman through and through and his interest went far beyond his day to day work, extending from miniature railways through narrow gauge to the most obscure industrial railways. Ray travelled the length and breadth of the British Isles and many locations abroad in pursuit of his subject.

Thankfully for us, and indeed future generations, Ray was also an accomplished photographer. His extensive collection has been kept complete and forms an important part of the photographic archives of *The* NOSTALGIA *Collection*.
So many people have helped - with snippets and guidance, facts and information - space, and space alone, precludes mention of them all, so THANK YOU ALL!

Dedication

John Axon GC

4 December 1900 - 9 February 1957

John Axon was a driver based at Stockport Edgeley shed (9B). On 7 February 1957 he was tragically killed while driving Class 8F No 48188 on the the 11.05 Buxton to Warrington Freight consisting of 33 wagons and a guards van. On approaching a downward gradient near Chapel-on-le-Frith Driver Axon was applying the brakes to stop the train, prior to descending the gradient, when the steam pipe supplying the brakes fractured. Scalding hot steam escaping from the pipe filled the cab and prevented any remedial action being taken to seal the pipe. The resulting loss of the steam brakes, meant the only course of action was to apply the handbrake and pin down the wagon brakes by hand. Driver Axon applied the hand brake and instructed the fireman to jump from the locomotive and apply as many wagon brakes as possible. - which he bravely did, With the train now rolling down the gradient and gathering speed, due to the limited braking available being insufficient to stop the 750+ ton runaway, Driver Axon remained on the footplate to warn the signalman at Dove Holes thereby enabling the evacuation of a DMU at Chapel-on-le-Frith. Sadly there was not time to clear a Rowsley to Stockport freight from the runaway's path and the two collided resulting in the death of Driver Axon and the guard of the freight train John Creamer.

John Axon was awarded the George Cross in recognition of his bravery. A Commemorative plaque has been placed on the station at Chapel-on-le-Frith.

Introduction

1957 was the year that saw the dawn of the manned space flight - or to be more precise the 'dogged' space flight. Russia were to send the first living creature from earth into space when a dog called Laika left earth in Sputnik II. The USA meanwhile were dogged with problems when their first flight blew up on the launch pad.

In music the pop charts were becoming ever more popular as the teenagers of the day began to tune in increasingly to the thinking that everyone had to know what was top of the charts in order to gain street cred! The transistor radio, the first of which had been released just 3 years earlier was beginning to be noticed and would explode during the 1960's when prices became affordable for the masses. This in turn fuelled the hit parade's popularity like nothing else.

Hits of the year incuded two versions of *Singing the blues* from Guy Mitchell and Tommy Steele, *Young Love* by Tab Hunter ran away with the top spot from late February through to mid April, while Lonny Donnegan was *Putting on the style* during June/July and Elvis was topping the charts with *All shook up* in high summer.
The Second World War had finished over a decade ago but the intervening years had been tough going as the country went through the process of recovery. But as 1957 dawned there was a feeling of renewed optimism, bomb sites had largely been cleared and new building was increasingly under way. The first of the Prefabs, over 150,000 of which had been built in Britain after the war, were in theory reaching the end of their intended life span. The Prefab however had taken root in many peoples hearts and examples can still be found today. Indeed in 2002 there were still over 600 in Bristol alone!

For many 1957 would be the first year that they could afford a family holiday and of course this was before the Motor Car had become virtually every family's possession. Travel was therefore by coach or by rail. *Royal Blue, Grey Green, Tilling, Black & White, Midland Red, Crosville, Standerwisck...* were but just a few of the many companies whose coaches criss crossed the country. Coach Stations were strategically placed on a busy network of routes, many a reader will no doubt recall changing coaches at such places as Victoria in London, Digbeth in Birmingham and of course Cheltenham where as a youngster one of your authors thought you simply had to go irrespective of where you had come from or where you were going!

The railway was of course the preferred means of travel for most, but price was, as now, a major consideration in 1957. In 1957, although you could still reach so many places by train, this was before the Beeching Era of mass closures. *Ilfracombe, Padstow, Perranporth, Kingsbridge, Brixham, Hunstanton, Bridport, Porthcawl, Cardigan, Coniston...* the list would fill a book! Suffice to say you could even go to *California* by train - on the erstwhile route from North Walsham to Great Yarmouth (closed just two years later) - as one of your authors did and proudly told all his junior school chums!

Looking back now, and in particular with the prospect that climate change will bring a need to change our collective ways, 1957 could well be the last year the UK had a railway network that, had it been fully utilised, maintained and developed could have provided a real alternative to the hell that are our roads today!

Peter Townsend
Northamptonshire

John Stretton
Oxfordshire

February 2008

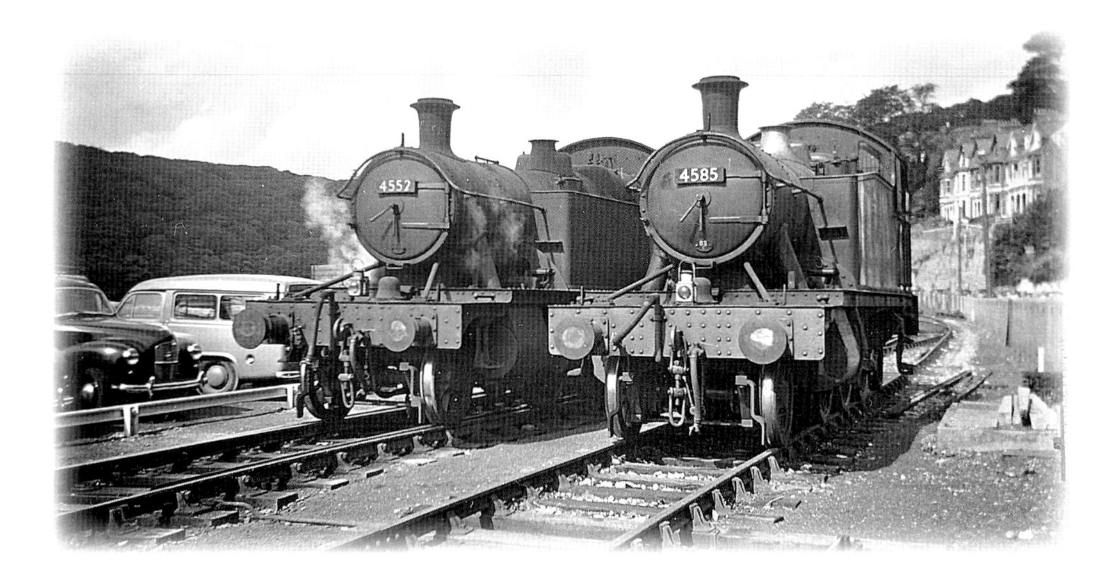

Above: **LOOE** Another popular holiday destination, especially for day trips. Reached by rail from Liskeard station, on the GWR main line in Cornwall, visitors to the branch would be treated to a trip taking them under that line and making a reversal at Coombe Junction station, mid-way along the line. Two ex-GWR 2-6-2Ts stand at the end of the branch line from Liskeard in September, close to the site of the old engine shed, awaiting their trains back to Liskeard. No 4552, left, was based at St Blazey shed for the whole of its BR life, for just such a service, until its withdrawal on 9 September 1961. Its companion No 4585 did not arrive at St Blazey until 17 May 1952, from Swindon shed; its end came on 3 October 1959.

Oppsite page **COOMBE JUNCTION** No 4585 has travelled up the branch from Looe and has uncoupled from the carriages and has set forward towards the short head shunt. Once clear of the points she will run back towards the camera, the signalman having reset the points, down the left hand line to run round the stock. Once recoupled on the other end she will travel a short distance from whence she came before diverging to the left for the climb up to Liskeard

Inset: **LISKEARD** No 4585 is now making that climb up from Coombe Junction towards Liskeard. Once it has passed under the viaduct the train will climb through 180 degrees before reaching the branch platform at Liskeard.

Steam on the Western Region

4954

Opposite: **BANBURY** The steam railway had many practices that have disappeared in these 'high tech' days! One such, was the pre-dominance of station pilots, scattered through-out the land, to lie in wait for the call to help out in some emergency. Largely the preserve of smaller locomotives, there were perforce occasions when 'main line' motive power was pressed into service and this is the case here, as '4900 Hall' Class No 4954 *Plaish Hall* handles a period of shunting in Banbury station on 12 March. A much-travelled engine in its 15 years of BR life, it is here allocated to Oxford shed. The end came at Oxley (Wolverhamp-ton) on 29 November 1964.

Below: **FOWEY** The railway originally arrived in Fowey on 1 June 1869 with a branch from Lostwithiel by the Cornwall Railway. A second branch, from Par by the Cornwall Minerals Railway arrived exactly five years later and the two became linked, giving a 'circular' route from the GW main line. Life was not uncomplicated, however, leading to changes of ownership before the GWR inherited services and traffic gradually declined, with the result that the first stretch from Lostwithiel lost its passenger services on 4 January 1965 and the whole of the Par branch closed on 1 July 1968. In September 1957 '1400' Class 0-4-0 No 1419 waits to leave the station for a trip to Par.

1957 Happenings (1)

Prime Minister Anthony Eden steps down
The Suez crisis influences decision *9 January*

Harold Macmillan new Prime Minister
Beats favourite Rab Butler *10 January*

Liverpool's Cavern Club opens
Made famous by The Beatles appearances *16 January*

Dwight D Eisenhower (34th US President)
inaugerated for 2nd Term *20 January*

Railway Accident (See *John Axon* Page 2)
Freight train runs away *9 February*

TV between 6pm and 7pm
The so called 'Toddlers Truce' ends allowing broadcasts in this 'Childrens bedtime' hour *February*

British Railways order
30 new D800 Warship locos *February*

Andrei Gromyko appointed
Soviet Foreign Minister *15 February*

Ghana gains independence
formerly Gold Coast & British Togoland *6 March*

Suez Canal
reopened by Egypt *8 March*

EEC formed
The Treaty of Rome signed *25 March*

Brecon Beacons
becomes a National Park *17 April*

Ffestiniog Railway
New halt opened at Pen y Bryn *20 April*

Petrol Rationing in UK ends
introduced due to Suez crisis *14 May*

NEWBURY Opened on 21 December 1847 by the GWR, Newbury was from its earliest days a busy place, with, at its height, having a branch to Lambourn and being on the Didcot, Newbury & Southampton Railway through route, as well as being on the original main line from Paddington to the West Country, serving both local areas and far-flung destinations. In an undated view, No 3211 stands patiently in one of the main line platforms, but waiting to take passengers to more local places. Introduced by Collett in the 1930s, the '2251' Class 0-6-0 was a truly versatile type and saw employment of all manner of duties. No 3211 was new in March 1948, to Didcot shed and it proudly wears that depot's shedplate on the smokebox in this view. A move to Newport (Ebbw Junction) came on 28 Janaury 1961, with withdrawal there on 8 September 1962. *MJS collection*

Left: **MONMOUTH TROY**
12 October saw centenary celebrations of the railway between Usk and Monmouth. The Stephenson Locomotive Society (Midland Area) ran a half day special for enthusiasts to celebrate the occasion, leaving Pontypool Road station at 12.45 p.m. The eighteen mile run to Monmouth was scheduled to take two hours ten minutes and the train is seen here on arrival, behind ex-GWR '5700' Class 0-6-0PT No 4668. A mere fifteen minutes was allocated to 'see the sights' and the tour participants are here scurrying around the station to soak up the atmosphere and take their photographs. Looking northwest, the line branching to the right and over the river Wye on a short viaduct, beyond the water tower, ultimately led to Chepstow, whilst the way ahead and then swinging to the left, to again cross the Wye, was the line to Ross on Wye. Today this view looks at the main A40 roadway running on the old trackbed. *Gerald Adams/MJS collection*

Above left: **PENZANCE** 'County' Class 4-6-0 No 1006 *County of Cornwall* stands by the tall, instantly recognisable wall at Penzance station, waiting for a return run towards Devon and, ultimately, Paddington. Designed by Hawksworth in 1945, to supplement and update the ailing GWR express fleet, the 'Counties' were a departure from accepted Swindon practice and were not universally liked by crews. However, this may have been down to prejudice and/or unwillingness to learn new 'tricks', rather than anything inherently wrong with the design! No 1006's chimney adorned a garden in Cam for the 42 years following withdrawal but has now been donated by owner John Fryer to 'The County 1014 *County of Glamorgan* Project', which aims to recreate one of the class from parts of

other locomotives! It spent most of its latter years in Devon/Cornwall before moving to 82C (Swindon) in mid-December 1962, from where the end came on 28 September 1963.

Right: **DAWLISH WARREN** A small habitation compared to neighbouring Dawlish, admittedly, but the Warren had long platforms to accommodate major holiday expresses bringing hundreds of holidaymakers here every summer. Eschewing the central through roads, '4073 Castle' Class 4-6-0 No 4037 *The South Wales Borderers* swings into the platform and slows for the stop, en route to Plymouth in July, watched by a single parent and child. Although it spent much time at Devon and Cornwall sheds after 1956, it is here shedded to Landore (Swansea) and it would be interesting to know the actual working on this day! *MJS*

Left: **DAWLISH WARREN** Moving to the Dawlish end of the platform, I am watched closely by the porter as I stray beyond the normal public area to capture my portrait of '4900 Hall' Class 4-6-0 No 5999 *Wollaton Hall.* This time there are many more people around, as a healthy throng of pleasure seekers climb down from the carriages. A Taunton engine for much of its BR life and working from that shed in this view, a transfer to Westbury came on 7 October 1961, from where it saw out duties until 8 September 1962. Note the substantial wooden station buildings, providing waiting areas and toilet facilities. *MJS*

Below: **WEST OF ENGLAND Main Line** An unidentified 'County' Class 4-6-0 caught at speed - believed to be near Cullompton, Devon.

Below left: **DAWLISH** The sea wall at Dawlish is famous and countless thousands have walked along the elevated pathway above the beach between Dawlish and the Warren over the years. Again in July, '5101' Class 2-6-2T No 4156 has just passed that stretch and is slowing for the stop at Dawlish, with a local from Exeter to Newton Abbot. Unlike many of its contemporaries, No 4156 operated out of only two depots in the last fifteen years of its life – 86A (Newport [Ebbw Junction]) and 86E (Severn Tunnel Junction). It is a Newport loco when snapped here, working away from its more normal haunts. Note the tall houses on the cliff top, with their excellent sea views. *MJS*

Below right: **BRYNMAWR** A station on the erstwhile L&NWR line west from Abergavenny, as that railway attempted the encroach onto GWR territory, it was also at the head of the GW valley line to Aberbeeg and Newport. Despite the LMS connection, GWR 0-6-0PTs were a common sight at Brynmawr, especially on Auto trains such as this, with '6400' Class No 6408 about to restart its journey on 26 October. Here shedded at Merthyr – with an appropriate 88D shedplate – it spent much of its working days in South Wales, but did have brief excursions into England between March 1958 and June 1960. *Gerald Adams/MJS collection*

Steam in the the Midlands, the North, the South & Scotland

Above: **LEICESTER (Belgrave Road)** At the end of a long meandering branch, Leicester (Belgrave Road) station was the Great Northern Railway's incursion into the Midlands city. Originally intended to be on a through route striking westwards, this was as far as the company reached, opening on 2 October 1882. Out of the city centre and serving predominantly rural areas, ordinary passenger traffic was never great and these ceased on 7 December 1953, leaving just freight to local outlets and holiday traffic to the East Coast – usually Skegness or Mablethorpe – to continue into the 1960s. Thus, for much of the year after 1953, the huge site sat empty. Things were enlivened, however, in June 1957, when an exhibition to help celebrate the Midland Railway centenary was held here. On 20 June, preserved ex-Midland Railway locos 4-2-2 No 118 (LMS No 673) and 2-4-0 No 158A are seen in the bay platform, for public inspection, with children gaining entry for the grand sum of 6d! *MJS collection*

Below: **NOTTINGHAM (Midland)** Nottingham was once home to three separate railways – Great Northern, Great Central and Midland. The latter railway's station was on one of the main routes to London (St Pancras) from Leeds and Sheffield and was itself approached by a multiplicity of lines. One such was a branch travelling northeast to Newark and Lincoln and a service bound for this route is seen in the platform on 27 April, behind 'D16' Class 4-4-0 No 62535. A widely travelled locomotive, it had been transferred to Lincoln shed a mere seven days prior to this view and, therefore, would probably have been a 'cop' to local spotters! Sadly, it was withdrawn less than eight months after this scene, on 14 December. *MJS collection*

1957 Happenings (2)

Stanley Matthews
Plays last game for England against Denmark away England won 4-1 *15 May*

The FA Cup *4 May*
Aston Villa win
Aston Villa 2 - 1 Manchester United

Wimbledon
Lew Hoad beats Ashley Hooper to win Men's Singles Final: 6-2, 6-1, 6-2
Althea Gibson beats Darlene Hard to win Women's Singles Final: 6-3, 6-2 *July*

The Derby
Won by Crepello ridden by Lester Piggott *6 June*

The Grand National
Won by Sundew ridden by Fred Winter *April*

Formula One
Juan Manuel Fangio driving for Maserati wins his fifth drivers championship

Cricket
Surrey win the County Championship
England beat the West Indies 3 wins 2 draws

SALISBURY There were many locations around the UK where trains had an engine change and/or saw services handled by locomotives of differing regions. Salisbury, on the main line to the West Country out of Waterloo, was home to both areas of interest and was a spotter's delight. On 13 July, No 30732 backs onto to an express bound for Exeter (Central), as the shunter shares some amusing pleasantry with the driver! One of the ageing Class 'T9' 4-4-0 locomotives, introduced by Drummond for the L&SWR in 1899 and affectionately known as 'Greyhounds', this engine spent its latter years alternating between London and Portsmouth area sheds and here wears a 70F shedplate, denoting that its current home is at Fratton. Withdrawal was from Eastleigh on 22 October 1959. Note the substantial brick built signalbox.
Gerald Adams/MJS collection

73154

PERTH was at the conflux of Caledonian Railway lines from the southwest, west, north and east, as well as North British routes from south and east. Thus the town and railway tended to grow together, with the result that a large engine shed was duly established immediately to the south of the station, which housed 138 locos in 1950. Though seen here restarting on a southbound express, 'Class 5' 4-6-0 No 73154 was not one of Perth's own. New in June 1957, it is seen just a few months later when working from its home shed of Glasgow St Rollox (65B). Heads poke from the carriages and other travellers wait on this platform and that to Dundee, to the right. *MJS collection*

Left: **BLOXHAM** As seen from the A361 roadbridge, a bright day in April shows off the station site to advantage, presenting a delightful scene so redolent of similar wayside halts throughout the erstwhile GWR. Neatly tended garden and vegetable patch complement the equally tidy permanent way, platforms and approach roadway. Passengers no longer gather for trains, however, since 4 June 1951, with only a limited freight service providing revenue. This, too, ended, on 4 November 1963, leading to eventual track reclamation and demolition of all evidence of the railway. Today, the site is unrecognisable, as this view is submerged beneath a housing development following the line of the track and also covering the goods yard. *MJS collection*

Inset: **SHIPLEY** On a dull and wet but unidentified day in 1957, No 40147 pauses at Shipley station for waiting passengers to board the Leeds-Bradford train. Lying to the east of the town centre, this station was built in the late 19th century, some 500 yds south of the original one from 1846 and the area has seen many developments over the years. Currently electrified, the large canopies have gone and the whole has a much more open air. One of Stanier's 1935-designed Class '3' 2-6-2Ts for just such local traffic as this, 40147 was shedded at Manningham (Bradford) at this date and spent the whole of its BR life in the Leeds/Bradford/Wakefield areas. Withdrawal was on 15 December 1962 from the last named. *MJS collection*

THE LICKEY INCLINE climbing from Bromsgrove to Blackwell, on the ex-LMS route south of Birmingham, has long been the steepest sustained main line railway incline in the UK. At two miles and an incline of 1-in-37, it provides a stern challenge even today, to the 21st century's more powerful motive power, but in the halcyon days of steam, it was a major obstacle. Engines were allocated to Bromsgrove shed purely for the purposes of banking trains up the gradient. One particularly powerful engine – affectionately known as Big Bertha – was built specifically for the job, but more often than not multiple locos were used. This is the case here, as ex-GWR '9400' Class 0-6-6PTs Nos 8404 and 8401 put their muscle behind a northbound express on 13 April. Uncoupled to the train, the locos would simply drop off the back when reaching the summit, to then return to the foot of the climb to await the next job. *Gerald Adams/MJS collection*

HALL GREEN is the next stop from Yardley Wood, on the journey to Birmingham. The station boasted an extensive goods yard and some of this can be glimpsed beyond the train in this view looking north on 8 June. One of five '3100' Class ex-GWR 2-6-2T locomotives rebuilt by Collett in 1938 from Churchward's '3150' Class introduced in 1906, No 3101 spent most of its last years based at Tyseley, apart from a four week stay at Gloucester in November 1952 and was withdrawn just two months after this view. *Gerald Adams/MJS collection*

1957
Happenings (3)

The Copyright Act 1956 becomes law
Films and Broadcasts covered
for the first time under UK act *1 June*

The Watlington Branch
Last passenger trains runs on branch
from Princess Risborough *29 June*

Record June Temperature
35.6 degrees centigrade recorded
in London *29 June*

Britons 'Never had it so good'
Prime Minister Harold Macmillan's famous
speech delivered to fellow Conservatives in
Bedford meeting *20 July*

RAF Historic Flight formed
at Biggin Hill forerunner of The Battle of
Britain Memorial Flight *July*

Tunisia becomes a Republic
Habib Bourguiba first President *July*

International Atomic Energy Agency
The IAEA is established *29 July*

USA ends nuclear tests
2 year suspension announced *21 August*

Malaya gains independence
from United Kingdom *31 August*

Wolfenden Report published in UK
starts far reaching debate on
Gay and Lesbian issues *3 September*

King Haakon VII of Norway
dies and Olav V succeeds
to the throne *21 September*

Opposite: **YARDLEY WOOD** Situated on the GWR's Birmingham and North Warwick line, Yardley Wood was the third station south of Tyseley, opened in 1908, on the southern fringes of Birmingham; it provided a useful commuting and/or shopping facility, along with others on the route to the city centre from Warwick and Stratford-upon-Avon. On 8 June, '5101' Class 2-6-2T No 4125 slows for the stop as it enters the station, after the long straight stretch from the direction of Shirley, with just such a train bound for the city. Along with others in the 4122-29 number bloc, No 4125 was allocated to Birkenhead at the dawn of Nationalisation. A move to Tyseley for this work came in April 1957, but the stay was short-lived, with yet another move south, this time to Severn Tunnel Junction shed on the eastern edge of South Wales in November. *Gerald Adams/MJS collection*

Below: **SHIRLEY** Initially not one of the busiest stations on the line, partly due to its more rural local character, this did change over the years up to and after WWII as development south of Birmingham grew. Some of that more bucolic nature can be seen in this portrait of the location on 8 June, as '5101' Class 2-6-2T No 4127 waits to depart south with a typical three-coach train for local services. This was another of the class imported from Birkenhead for the summer of 1957, before departing to Severn Tunnel Junction in November. Withdrawal came on 9 February 1963 from that shed. *Gerald Adams/MJS collection*

BRITISH
RAILWAYS
BORDESLEY
GENERAL

Right: **BORDESLEY** Prior to the introduction of what are now often referred to as 'Heritage' DMUs, front ends of diesel motive power were devoid of any additional adornment other than the paintwork of the whole body. Even into the 1960s, many of the SR's EMUs were still in this state, but the DMUs introduced from the 1955 modernisation programme were daubed with an ever-growing volume of yellow paint. Supposedly to warn of approaching trains – and the Health & Safety Executive maintain this stance even today – it is arguable that very few lives have been saved due to this precaution. Certainly, many other countries do not see the need, including the USA, where litigation is rife. In hindsight, the most attractive of these warnings were the 'whiskers', as demonstrated in this view of a pairing of brand new Derby 'Suburban' 3-car Class 116s, rounding the curve at Bordesley, on crew training duties on 14 September. Note the 'white-walled tyres'! *Gerald Adams/MJS collection*

Left: **BORDESLEY** Swinging left through 45° from the view of the new DMUs, another busy scene is captured on 31 August. Smoke drifts casually from '9F' Class 2-10-0 No 92048 as it moves yet another mixed freight train over the ex-LMS cross-Birmingham line between Castle Bromwich and Barnt Green. Part of the ex-Midland cross country route from Derby to Bristol, it is here traversing the ex-GWR main line from Birmingham (Snow Hill) to the south and, ultimately, Paddington. Strategically placed on the southern edge of Birmingham, Bordesley was graced with a large warehouse and generous expanse of sidings and both are glimpsed in this view looking north, with a diesel shunter gainfully employed. *Gerald Adams/MJS collection*

Above: **LEICESTER Midland Shed** Initially a single roundhouse was provided by the Midland Counties Railway from 5 July 1840. Subsequent widening of the main line necessitated part of this to be removed and a second roundhouse was added, on the opposite side of the building to the main line, in 1855. A brick built, 3-road dead-end shed was added close to this newer roundhouse in 1893 and further improvements continued in the yard thereafter. Work began in 1944 to completely remodel the site, with earlier buildings demolished and a completely new roundhouse provided in 1945, together with the coaling plant and attendant buildings seen

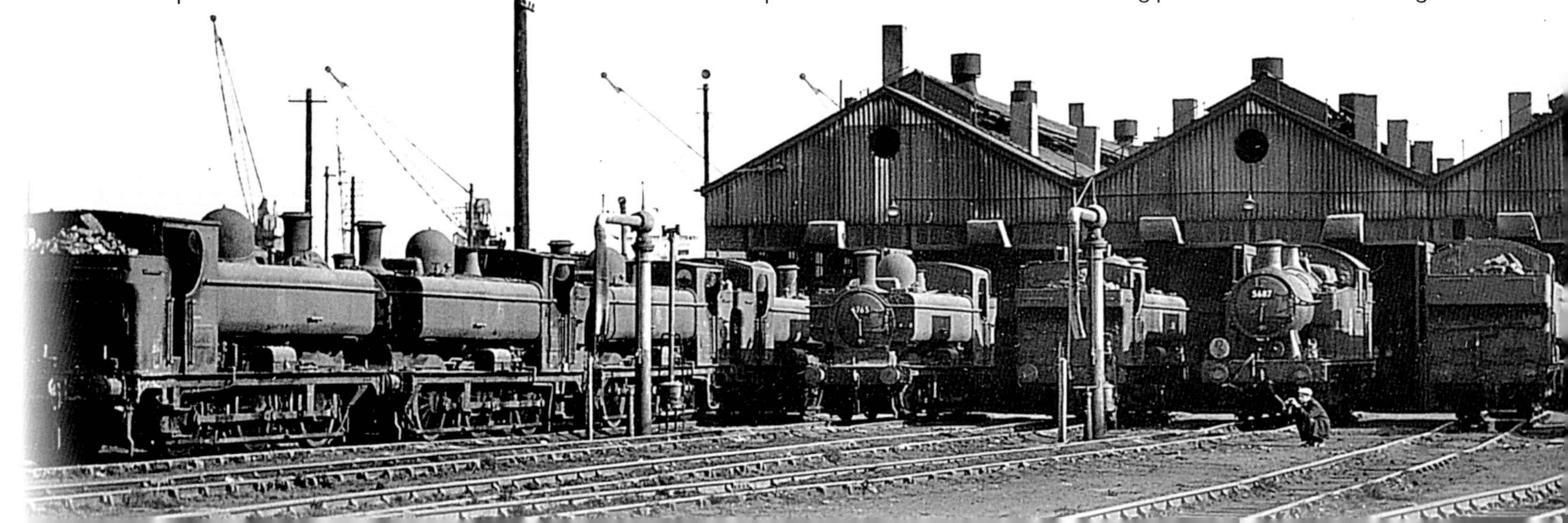

LOCOS ON SHED

Four shed views, from three different regions and with locos in different degrees of cleanliness!

here. It closed to steam on 13 June 1965, but continued as a diesel servicing depot, with the roundhouse demolished in 1970. The site and basic facilities survived into 2007, but with most of its previous function no longer required. On 6 August, '8F' Class 2-8-0 No 48380, of Kettering shed, has been coaled and watered and waits for a return south. *MJS collection*

Above middle: **EASTLEIGH** Undoubted star of the show is SR 'King Arthur' 4-6-0 No 30793 *Sir Ontzlake*, Fresh out of overhaul at the neighbouring Works on 9 July and waiting to return to its home at Stewart's Lane shed, it stands in pristine condition between 'M7' Class 0-4-4T No 30029 and a Bullied 'Pacific'. New in 1926 and named after one of the Knights of Arthurian legend, it was dispensed with at Basingstoke shed on 24 September 1962. *MJS collection*

left: **CARDIFF CANTON** The original shed at Canton was a 6-road, dead end affair, with slated northlight pattern roof and opened in 1882 to replace the much smaller facility provided in 1872 south of Roath station. A brick built roundhouse was added to the south side in 1897 and further improvements were made in 1925 and 1931. With an allocation in 1950 of 102 – including many express locomotives for the run to London – it closed to steam on 10 September 1962, to then be converted to diesel operation and it was still open in 2007, but in a much reduced form.. On 14 April, '1500' Class 0-6-0PT No 1508 and '2251' Class 0-6-0 No 2203 wait for their respective calls of duty. *Gerald Adams/MJS collection*

Below left: **CARDIFF EAST DOCK** Built by the GWR during the major investment in its system in the early 1930s, the shed opened in 1931 and was predominantly replacing and built on the site of the ex-Rhymney Railway buildings that dated from 1901. It boasted eight roads to a dead end shed and had an allocation of 62 in 1950. Seen here on 14 April, the impressive array of ex-GWR tanks facing the camera includes (l-r) '5700' Class 0-6-0PT No 6765, '5600' Class 0-6-2T No 5687, '5700' Class 0-6-0PT No 4626, and '9400' Class 0-6-0PT No 9437. Later years would see it house much larger engines. It closed on 2 August 1965 – the last stem shed in the area – and was subsequently demolished. Note the photographer squatting for his personal take on the scene. *Gerald Adams/MJS collection*

1957 No 1 Records

January	
Singing the blues	*Guy Mitchell*
Singing the blues	*Tommy Steele*
Singing the blues	*Guy Mitchell*
The Garden of Eden	*Frankie Vaughan*
February	
The Garden of Eden	*Frankie Vaughan*
Singing the blues	*Guy Mitchell*
The Garden of Eden	*Frankie Vaughan*
Young Love	*Tab Hunter*
March	
Young Love	*Tab Hunter*
April	
Young Love	*Tab Hunter*
Cumberland Gap	*Lonnie Donegan*
May	
Cumberland Gap	*Lonnie Donegan*
Rock-A-Billy	*Guy Mitchell*
Butterfly	*Andy Williams*
June	
Yes Tonight Josephine	*Johnnie Ray*
Gamblin man/Putting on the style	*Lonnie Donnegan*
July	
Gamblin man/Putting on the style	*Lonnie Donnegan*
All shook up	*Elvis Presley*
August	
All shook up	*Elvis Presley*
Diana	*Paul Anka*
September	
Diana	*Paul Anka*
October	
Diana	*Paul Anka*
November	
That'll be the day	*The Crickets*
Mary's boy child	*Harry Belafonte*
December	
Mary's boy child	*Harry Belafonte*

Below: **DOVER** Oliver Bullied was certainly unconventional in his locomotive design, when his 'Merchant Navy' Pacifics first appeared in 1941 and his notion of numbering was also unique, including as it did an element of the wheel arrangement! With chain driven valve gear and a partially welded boiler and firebox, as opposed to the more normal riveted design, he was an innovator, but it was his radical approach to streamlining that was the most obvious departure from accepted practice. Originally numbered 21C1 by the Southern Railway, class leader 4-6-2 No 35001 *Channel Packet*, seen on Dover shed, received this more usual number in October 1949. Elements of the design did not find favour with crews and/or operational staff, to the end that many of the class were rebuilt to more standard shape, including No 35001 in August 1959. The expenditure was not wholly economic, however, as withdrawal came in November 1964, as dieselisation and further electrification on the SR took over the loco's duties. *MJS collection*

Below: **KING'S CROSS** Otherwise affectionately known as 'Top Shed', King's Cross shed was home to a wide variety of motive power, not least the superb Gresley 'Pacifics'. One such, 'A1' Class 4-6-2 No 60156 *Great Central* – complete with company crest on the smoke deflector – stands while receiving water in the yard in November, with newly arrived diesel shunter D3443 next to it. New on 25 October 1949, a Peppercorn development of Thompson's 1945 design, No 60156 was initially allocated to 'the Cross', leaving in September 1951 and returning in September 1956. Other homes were New England (Peterborough), Doncaster and York, before the final curtain on 22 May 1965. Sadly, none were preserved, but a totally new build of the design was reaching the latter stages in 2007 and No 60163 *Tornado*, taking the next sequential number from the originals, will indeed be a 'sight for sore eyes' when it is finally in steam! *MJS collection*

WATH Having an entry in the Domesday book, Wath-upon-Dearne, to give it its full title, has had various claims to fame over the years, including a racecourse, pottery and deep-mined coal but, for railway aficionados, it was the entrance of rail taking over from the local canal that really sparked its more recent importance. A huge marshalling yard was established in the north of the town with this and the depot's presence at the eastern end of the famed 'Woodhead Line' becoming legendary. The trans-Pennine overhead

electrified line was ahead of its time, juiced by 1500 volts DC in 1954 because of the steep gradients and difficulties for steam locomotion. Withdrawal of passenger services in 1970, the downturn in coal traffic across the Pennines and the impending cost of maintaining and upgrading the electrified route that was now unique on UK railways, all sounded the death knell, however and final closure came on 17 July 1981. The route was mothballed in the hope of restoration but, thus far, this has not been achieved, despite many rumours and ideas put forward. Today some of the route is open to walkers and cyclists. On 28 July, Wath depot is home to 'EM1' Class Bo-Bo's Nos 26040 and 26022 as a group of enthusiasts take advantage of access. *A R Goult/MJS collection*

Above: **OLD OAK COMMON** Situated around two miles west of Westbourne Park station and predominantly serving services into and out of Paddington, the shed was opened on 17 March 1906. Boasting a stud of 197 locomotives in 1950, it was one of the largest sheds in the country and a Mecca for enthusiasts, although a difficult place to visit without proper authority! It closed to steam 22 March 1965, but continues to this day as a diesel facility. Here with the early British Railways 'Lion and Wheel' emblem on the tender, 'King' Class 4-6-0 No 6011 *King James I* stands ready for the fray. Allocated to Wolverhampton (Stafford Road) shed at this time, it has 'Brum 0 Man 5' scrawled on the smokebox! New in April 1928 and fitted with double chimney in May 1956, it was withdrawn on 9 February 1963. *MJS collection*

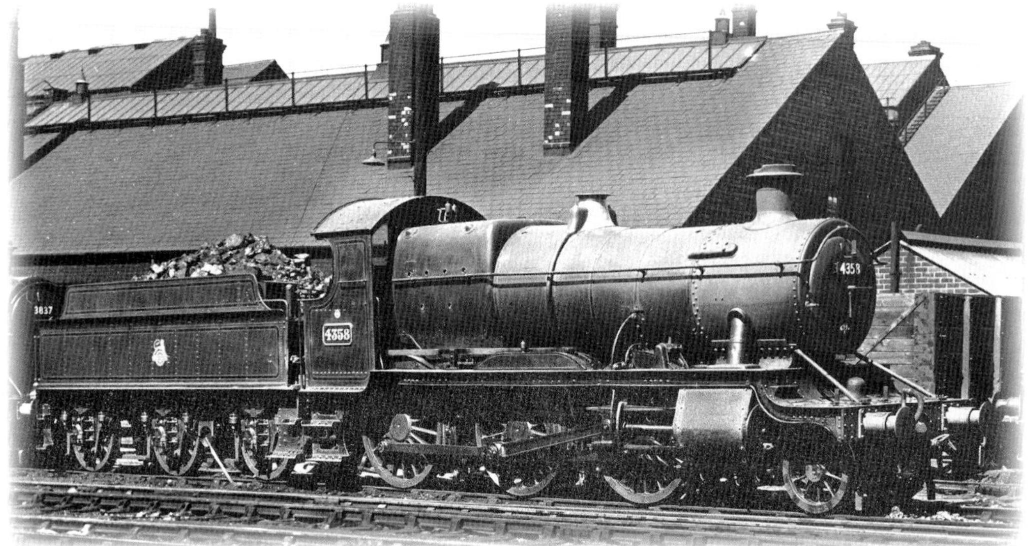

Above: **SWINDON** Looking clean and smart in its lined livery, it looks as though '4300' Class 4-6-0 No 4358 had also recently received attention at the nearby Works. Having moved from Neyland in deepest southwest Wales to Gloucester, two years before this view, it is possible that the new 'owner' was appreciative of some remedial attention. Its end was relatively nigh, however, on 8 August 1959. *MJS collection*

Below: **LEICESTER MIDLAND** Decidedly the more work-stained of the trio, an unidentified 'Standard Class 5' stands in the shed yard between duties. This view, from the deliciously named 'Birdcage' overlooking the shed and its yard, was a favourite haunt of your photographer...there was always something new to see! Note the large, post-War coaling stage and the proliferation of railway 'furniture' – lamp standards, semaphore signals, signalbox, goods wagons and telegraph wires! *MJS*

LEICESTER MIDLAND Another view from the 'Birdcage', this time looking towards the large roundhouse constructed in 1945. With an allocation of over 70 at its height and always plenty of visiting locomotives, 15C was a spotter's Mecca. In this view there is an impressive array of motive power, including Nos 40472, 45267, 42373, 75059 and 44163. Never an easy place to 'bunk', your photographer was successful on many occasions in avoiding the Foreman's attentions, but equally was thrown out on more than one visit! All that is left of this view in 2008 are the low squat building seen just encroaching into the centre right of the picture, beyond 75059, and some of the rails! *MJS*

OUT ON THE LINES

Below: **LEICESTER Knighton Cattle Dock** The crew of Standard Class '4' 2-6-0 No 76086 seem keen to have their photograph taken. The consist of three horse boxes and the men working behind would indicate that some shunting manoeuvres are taking place. One hopes that the men are not shovelling any erstwhile contents of the three wagons, or if they are that a station rose bed might benefit! *J F Clay / MJS Collection*

Above: **BRACKLEY** At its height, the historic market town of Brackley boasted two railway stations. One was on the erstwhile Great Central Railway, from Marylebone to the north and the second was a much more rural affair, being on the ex-L&NWR branch to Banbury (Merton Street) from Buckingham and Verney Junction. On 12 March, 79901, one of just two of this DMBS type built at BR's Derby Works, prepares to restart on its journey from Buckingham to Banbury. Built in August 1956, it was withdrawn from Bletchley depot in December 1966, after a very short active life. Note the large front cab windows and the station staff at this small wayside station.

This page: **BELGRAVE & BIRSTALL** The Great Central Railway was cruelly killed off by BR and has been mourned ever since by public and rail enthusiasts alike.

Happily, the preservationists of the current GCR have managed to save and restore much of the old infrastructure between this location and Loughborough (Central) some dozen or so miles to the north. Sadly, largely due to vandalism during the closure period, the attractive station at Belgrave & Birstall was swept away, but at least trains still run to this site, now called Leicester North.

On 24 April, a slightly unusual motive power type has been employed on this relatively short mixed freight. Heading south towards Leicester, an impressively clean 'K3' Class 2-6-0 No 61975 was an Annesley (Nottingham) loco at this date but it was to move north to Leeds in 1959, for its last two years of life. One of your authors would sit for hours on this fencing, while his grandfather tended his allotment, just off to the right of this view! *Geoff King/MJS collection*

Below: **LEICESTER Knighton Tunnel** A delight in steam days and one wholly absent today was the headboard worn by locomotives at the head of crack expresses. The midland main line north from St Pancras boasted two major services – The Thames-Clyde Express (from, not surprisingly, London to Glasgow) and The Palatine. Originally given by the LMS to an express between London and Manchester in 1938, it was suspended for the War but resurrected afterwards. Pre-War it ran as the 10.30 a.m. from London and 4.25 p.m. return, but post-War timings were changed to 7.55 a.m. and 2.25 p.m. With a journey time of 3 hrs 55 mins., there were stops at Leicester, Derby, Matlock, Millers Dale and Chinley. On an unidentified date in October, 'Jubilee' Class 4-6-0 No 45679 *Armada* bursts from Knighton Tunnel and passes the ancient ticket platform as it approaches the Leicester stop. *J F Clay/MJS collection*

Right: **WEST COAST MAIN LINE** Long before the wires went up, the ex-L&NWR route out of Euston was a major expressway, frequently known as 'The Premier Line'. Sadly, this image has no details of location or date in 1957, but it still shows what main line expresses were all about – a top link locomotive and eleven coaches at speed. Class leader 4-6-0 No 46100 *Royal Scot* coasts along a straight stretch, heading for London, allocated to 1B (Camden), from where it handled major expresses for many years up to 7 November 1959, when it was 'downgraded' to Nottingham shed, to handle

the less prestigious Midland Main Line trains between there and St Pancras. It survived there – apart from a two month stay at Derby in the summer of 1961 – until withdrawal on 3 November 1962. Happily, it was saved from destruction, complete with nameplate commemorating its North American tour of 1933 but, in reality, the engine seen here and saved for the nation is not the original, but No 6152 *The King's Dragoon Guardsman*. Both were in Crewe Works at the time of her American adventure and 6100 was not ready for the trip, so identities were changed 'to protect the innocent'!

1957 Arrivals & Departures

Births

Adrian Edmondson	*comedian*	24 January
Robert Townsend	*actor*	6 February
Gordon Strachan	*football manager*	9 February
Osama bin Laden	*Islamic leader*	10 March
Mal Donaghy	*footballer/coach*	17 March
Daniel Day-Lewis	*actor*	29 April
Jo Brand	*comedienne*	3 May
Sid Vicious	*musician*	10 May
Siouxsie Sioux	*singer*	27 May
Javid Miandad	*cricketer*	12 June
Anna Lindh	*politician (Sweden)*	19 June
Fern Britton	*TV presenter*	17 July
Robin Cousins	*figure skater*	17 August
Steve Davis	*snooker player*	22 August
Steven Fry	*author/actor/comedian*	24 August
Jane Torvill	*figure skater*	7 October
Dawn French	*comedienne*	11 October
Donny Osmond	*singer*	9 December

Deaths

Humphrey Bogart	*actor*	(b. 1899)	14 January
John Axon	*railwayman*	(b. 1900)	9 February
Eliot Ness	*FBI agent*	(b. 1903)	16 May
Oliver Hardy	*actor*	(b. 1892)	7 August
Jean Sibelius	*composer*	(b. 1865)	20 September
Louis Burt Mayer	*film producer*	(b. 1885)	29 October
William Haywood	*architect*	(b. 1876)	4 November

RAILWAY WORKS

Below: **BRIGHTON WORKS** were opened by the London & Brighton Railway in 1840, constructing its first locomotive in 1852 and continuing through to BR days. It closed in 1962. Like many other Works, dedicated engines were employed to shunt stock around the site and here is a spectacularly liveried example. Also known as DS377, 377S was originally a Stroudley 'Terrier', numbered 2635, one of those rebuilt in 1911 from the earlier 1872 design, with a Marsh boiler and extended smokebox. Renumbered to 32635 in 1959 and allocated to Brighton shed, it was withdrawn on 29 April 1963, but here, on 5 May 1957 it is still very much alive and in immaculate condition. *Gerald Adams/MJS collection*

Above left: **SWINDON WORKS** was a much bigger empire than Brighton, with a greater record of locomotive construction and also a longer period of operation. Opening on 2 January 1843, it transformed both the GWR and the town of Swindon, making it into one of the railway towns in the UK. Having had the honour of building the last steam locomotive for BR – Class '9F' 2-10-0 No 92220 *Evening Star* – the Works continued to service diesel locos and units until an untimely and cruel closure decision in 1985…at the time of the 150th anniversary celebrations of the GWR! On 25 August, 'Dukedog' Class 4-4-0 No 9011 stands in 'C' Shop, in the early stages of scrapping, so soon after being withdrawn from Swindon shed on 13 July! The outside frames of this loco had started life as 'Bulldog' Class No 3415 *George A Mills* and the boiler had come from one of the former 'Duke' Class 4-4-0s hence the Class name of 'Dukedog' *Michael Hale/MJS collection*

Above right: **SWINDON WORKS** Many of today's preserved locomotives are castigated by those who remember 'the good old days' as being too clean. As if to show that not all motive power was dull and dirty in those dark days of the 1950s, 'Castle' Class 4-6-0 No 5000 *Launceston Castle* is in pristine condition in the yard of Swindon Works on 16 June. Bearing the relatively new British Railways transfer on its tender, it stands awaiting a fire being lit in the boiler and the tender being filled with coal, before moving the very short distance to return to its home at the nearby engine shed. Several moves followed before withdrawal on 22 November 1964 from Oxley (Wolverhampton). Note the neatly sorted collection of chimneys from all manner of more ancient types.
Gerald Adams/MJS collection

WOLVERTON WORKS

Wolverton Works was established by the London and Birmingham Railway Company in the 1830s, at the midpoint of the 112 mile-long route from London to Birmingham. Becoming part of the London & North Western Railway in 1846, the Works grew in importance and locomotive building commenced. 1877 saw this activity concentrated at Crewe, with Wolverton becoming, over time, the largest carriage Works in the UK; and in 1901 it became the first Works to employ electricity for both lighting and powering machines.

To shunt stock around the Works, a number of 0-6-0STs were employed, being Webb versions of Ramsbottom's 'Special Tanks'. One – No.CD8 – was named Earlestown.

Above and left: Unidentified examples of the shunting engines are seen going about their work in June 1957. *Gerald Adams/MJS collection*

Left and above: **WOLVERTON WORKS** More views in and around the Works complex in June 1957, including, left upper, No. 8 Earlestown, sandwiched between two 'sister' locomotives. Rather ancient looking carriages are seen in the yard awaiting eventual disposal and inside the Works, receiving attention. *Gerald Adams/MJS collection*

WATERLOO Though not the first numbered, the whole Class is known by No 30453's soubriquet, *King Arthur*. Initially designed by Maunsell for the L&SWR in 1925, there were quickly many variations among the class members, not least to take account of the idiosyncrasies of the Eastern and Central sections of the Southern empire. Like many of the class, the last decade or so of *King Arthur's* railway life was spent at Salisbury shed, until withdrawal on 23 August 1961. Sadly, 4-6-0 No 30453 was not to survive the cutter's torch, but No 30777 *Sir Lamiel* did, making many trips on the main lines to areas never explored during normal service.

FOCUS ON WHITBY

WHITBY This view of the northeast holiday destination sees Class 'D49' 4-4-0 No 62731 *Selkirkshire* at the head of RCTS 'Yorkshire Coast Railtour' on 23 June. Mid-way through the tour, the special is seen at Whitby Town station shortly before the 7 p.m. departure, to make the return run to York via what is now the North Yorks Moors Railway. Note the tall arrival signal and the attractive window designs on the signalbox. A young spotter and his dad study the engine. *MJS collection*

WHITBY A busy time at Whitby station, viewed from across the wide expanse of platform. The 'new order' for passenger services locally – Met-Camm Class 111 – prepares to obey the signal and leave the platform, while the 'old order' busies itself on shunting duties. Class '3' 2-6-0 No 77012, centre in this view, was here three years old, having been introduced on 24 July 1954, initially to Darlington shed. Allocated to Whitby from November 1955 to December 1958, it had several changes of allocation before withdrawal on 15 July 1967. Though of a distinctly older design mode, Class 'L1' 2-6-4T No 67754 was not much older, having been new in British Railway's days, on 2 March 1949. Again initially to Darlington and seeing many moves during it lifetime, it was here in the employ of Middlesborough shed. The end for this locomotive came on 17 November 1962, from Low Moor shed. *MJS collection*

WHITBY The ruins of the Benedictine Abbey – founded in 657 AD – stand boldly on East Cliff, right, overlooking the town and the engine shed. Initially opened by the York & North Midland Railway on 6 June 1847, the facility was enlarged in 1868 and re-roofed in 1903. A 42ft turntable was originally installed, later increasing to 50ft and then, in 1936, to 60ft. The shed closed on 6 April 1959, but the building was still standing into the 1990s, used as a ships' chandlers. On this day, Class 'A8' No 69864 – originally built as a 4-4-4T, but rebuilt to 4-6-2T, as seen here, in June 1935 – can only find space in the shed yard, along with a classmate and other types. It survived until 5 November 1958. *MJS collection*

1957
Happenings (3)

Fire at Nuclear Plant
Graphite core fire at Windscale, Cumbria — *10 October*

The Vatican
Vatican Radio starts broadcasting — *26 October*

Battery Railcars for BR announced
by Sir Ian Bolton at Glasgow Press Conference (Nos 79998/9) for use on the Aberdeen to Ballater line — *15 October*

The Lovell Telescope
The Lovell Radio Telescope enters service at Jodrell Bank — *October*

Laika in space
Russians launch Sputnik II carrying Laika the first dog in space — *3 November*

Plane Crash on Isle of Wight
Solent flying boat on route from Southampton to Lisbon and Madeira crashes at Chessel Down — *15 November*

Lewisham Rail Crash
Cannon Street to Ramsgate Express colides with Charring Cross to Hayes EMU - 92 killed — *4 December*

First US Satellite fails to lift off
rocket explodes on launch pad — *6 December*

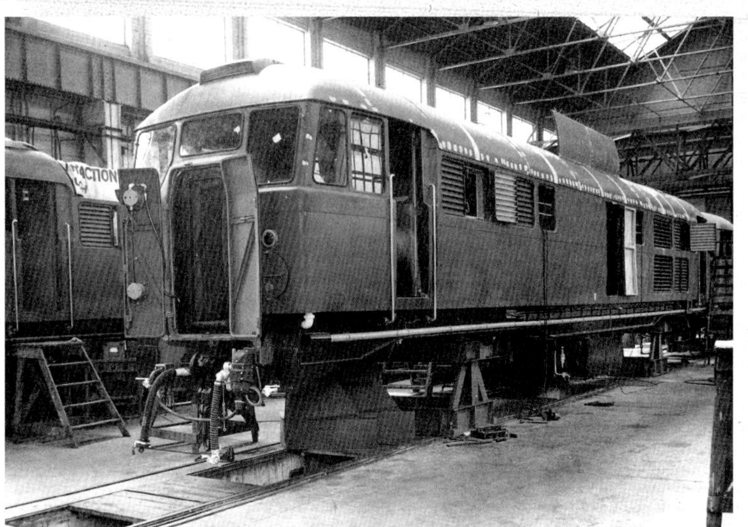

NANTYBWCH Situated on the ex-L&NWR branch from Abergavenny, in that railway's attempt to infiltrate the Welsh Valleys, Nantybwch was also the junction for a line to the west that split to run to Rhymney and also continued along the Head of Valleys route. Thus there were workings for LMS (and Ex-LNWR) locomotives into this GWR heartland

and one such is here seen behind No 49409 on 26 October. Normally a somewhat surprising choice for passenger workings, the '7F' 0-8-0s were often pressganged into all manner of duties, though most did not operate losing quite as much steam as this one! Approximately thirty years old at this date, 49409 soldiered on until 13 June 1959. Contraction began in the 1950s, with passenger diagrams ending south to Risca on 13 June 1960 and complete closure of the western link and Nantybwch station on the same day. Note the wooden posted semaphore signal and the delightful signalbox.

Inset opposite: **LOUGHBOROUGH** The new order! Prototype 'Brush Type 2' D5500 nearing completion inside Brush's Loughborough workshops. *Brush/MJS collection*

Index

Acknowledgements 48

DATES

1957

7 February 2
12 March 7, 34
April 1957 23
13 April 42
14 Apri 27
14 April 27
24 April 35
27 April 14
5 May 38
June 13, 17, 40, 41
8 June 21, 23
20 June 13
23 June 43
July 11, 12
9 July 27
13 July 15, 39
28 July 31
6 August 27
25 August 39
31 August 25
September 7
14 September 25
October 36
12 October 9
26 October 12, 47
November 29
14 December 14

Pre 1957

5 July 1840 26
2 January 1843 39
6 June 1847 45
21 December 1847 8
1 June 1869 7
2 October 1882 13
17 March 1906 31
April 1928 31
June 1935 45
2 March 1949 44
October 1949 28
25 October 1949 29
4 June 1951 19
September 1951 29
November 1952 21
17 May 1952 4
7 December 1953 13
24 July 1954 44
November 1955 44
May 1956 31
August 1956 34
September 1956 29

Post 1957

March 1958 12
5 November 1958 45
December 1958 44
6 April 1959 45
13 June 1959 47
August 1959 28
8 August 1959 32
3 October 1959 4
22 October 1959 15
7 November 1959 36
June 1960 12
13 June 1960 47
28 Janaury 1961 8
23 August 1961 42
9 September 1961 4
7 October 1961 11
8 September 1962 8, 11
10 September 1962 27
24 September 1962 27
3 November 1962 37
17 November 1962 44
December 1962 11
15 December 1962 19
9 February 1963 23, 31
29 April 1963 38
28 September 1963 11
4 November 1963 19
November 1964 28
22 November 1964 39
29 November 1964 7
4 January 1965 7
22 March 1965 31
22 May 1965 29
13 June 1965 27
2 August 1965 27
December 1966 34
15 July 1967 44
1 July 1968 7
17 July 1981 31

LOCOMOTIVES

BR

26022 31
26040 31
40147 19
60156 29
73154 17
75059 33
76086 35
92048 25
92220 *Evening Star* 39
D3443 29
DMBS 79901 34

Ex-GER

62535 14

Ex-GWR

1006 *County of Cornwall* 10
1014 *County of Glamorgan* 10
1419 7
1508 27
2203 27
3101 21
3211 8
3415 *George A Mills* 39
4037 *The South Wales Borderers* 11
4125 23
4127 23
4156 12
4358 32
4552 4
4585 4
4626 27
4668 9
4954 *Plaish Hall* 7
5000 *Launceston Castle* 39
5687 27
5999 *Wollaton Hall* 11
6011 *King James I* 31
6408 12
6765 27
9011 39
9437 27

Ex-L&SWR

30029 27
30453 *King Arthur* 42
30732 15
30777 *Sir Lamiel* 20
30793 *Sir Ontzlake* 27

Ex-LBSCR

2635 38
32635 38
377S 38
DS377 38

Ex-LMS

42373 33
44163 33
45267 33
45679 *Armada* 36
46100 *Royal Scot* 36
48380 27
6152 *The King's Dragoon Guardsman* 37
673 13

Ex-LNER

61975 35

Ex-LNWR

CD8 *Earlstown* 40

Ex-MR

118 13
158A 13
40472 33

Ex-SR

35001 *Channel Packet* 28

New build

60163 *Tornado* 29

PEOPLE

Axon, John 2
Creamer, John 2

PLACES

Banbury 7
Belgrave & Birstall 35
Bloxham 19
Bordesley 25
Brackley 34
Brighton Works 38
Carbis Bay 2
Cardiff Canton 27
Cardiff East Dock 27
Dawlish 12
Dawlish Warren 11
Dover 28
Eastleigh 27
Fowey 7
Hall Green 21
King's Cross 29
Leicester Belgrave Road 13
Leicester Knighton Tunnel 36
Leicester Midland Shed 26, 32
Leicester Knighton Cattle Dock 35
Lickey Incline 20
Liskeard 4
Looe 4
Loughborough 47
Monmouth 9
Nantybwch 46
Newbury 8
Nottingham (Midland) 14
Old Oak Common 31
Penzance 10
Perth 17
Salisbury 15
Shipley 19
Shirley 23
Swindon 32
Swindon Works 39
Waterloo 42
Wath 30
West Coast Main Line 36
Whitby 43, 44, 45
Wolverton Works 40, 41
Yardley Wood 23